Finding Light: A Guide to Overcoming Youth Depression

Monica M. Schneider

Copyright © Monica M. Schneider

All rights reserved. No part of this book may be reproduced, stored in a retrieval system, or transmitted in any form or by any means, electronic, mechanical, photocopying, recording, or otherwise, without the prior written permission of the copyright holder, except in the case of brief quotations embodied in critical reviews and certain other noncommercial uses permitted by copyright law.

Acknowledgment

We would like to express our heartfelt gratitude to everyone who contributed to the creation of this book on youth depression.

First and foremost, we extend our deepest appreciation to the adolescents who bravely shared their experiences and insights, enriching this book with their perspectives and wisdom. Your courage and resilience inspire us all.

We are also immensely grateful to the parents, educators, mental health professionals, and advocates who work tirelessly to support young people struggling with depression. Your dedication and compassion make a profound difference in the lives of adolescents and their families.

Special thanks to [Name of Contributors, if applicable], whose expertise and contributions enhanced the quality and depth of this book.

We are indebted to our readers for their interest in understanding and addressing youth depression. Your commitment to promoting mental health and well-being in young people is truly commendable.

Lastly, we would like to acknowledge the countless individuals and organizations dedicated to advancing mental health awareness, advocacy, and research. Your efforts pave the way for a brighter and more hopeful future for adolescents worldwide.

Thank you all for your unwavering support and commitment to making a positive impact on the lives of young people. Together, we can create a world where every adolescent feels valued, supported, and empowered to thrive.

CONTENT

introduction _____ 9

Understanding Youth Depression _____ 13

Signs and Symptoms _____ 19

The Impact of Social Media _____ 25

Navigating School and Academic Pressure _____ 30

Family Dynamics and Support Systems _____ 36

Coping Mechanisms and Self-Care Practices _____ 42

Seeking Professional Help: Therapy and Counseling _____ 46

Medication and Alternative Treatments _____ 53

Overcoming Stigma and Seeking Help _____ 58

Building Resilience and Emotional Strength _____ 62

Cultivating Healthy Relationships _____ 68

Finding Purpose and Meaning _____ 74

Mindfulness and Meditation Techniques _____ 78

Lifestyle Changes for Mental Wellness _____ 83

Embracing Hope and Moving Forward _____ 89

Introduction:

Adolescence stands out as a crucial stage in the complex fabric of the human experience, one that is characterised by the convergence of self-definition, growth, and discovery. But in the midst of all the unending opportunities and goals that come with being young, depression is a silent cloud that hangs over a lot of young people. The pressures and difficulties that young people encounter in today's fast-paced, globally connected world are constantly changing, and this has a significant negative influence on their mental health. "Finding Light: A Guide to Overcoming Youth Depression" shines as a beacon of understanding, compassion, and perseverance within this complex landscape of emotions and experiences.

Depression is a complex phenomena that is sometimes cloaked in stigma and misinformation, especially among young people. It goes beyond simple melancholy or hopelessness, penetrating deep into one's mind, upsetting everyday routines, and shattering the entire foundation of identity. The voyage can be especially difficult for teenagers crossing the turbulent terrain of adolescence, bearing down on the burden of familial relationships, societal pressures, scholastic expectations, and existential questions. It can seem impossible to find comfort, understanding, and hope when one is experiencing such intense inner turmoil.

"Finding Light" aims to lift the curtain of ignorance surrounding teenage depression by providing a sympathetic and knowledgeable viewpoint that shows the way towards recovery and resiliency. This manual is essentially a monument to the strength of information, empathy, and community in promoting mental health and creating a sense of belonging. This book is a helpful resource for teenagers navigating the maze of depression as well as their friends and supporters, thanks to the participation of psychologists, the sharing of personal experiences, and the offering of useful techniques.

The understanding that depression is a normal reaction to the complexity of human existence rather than a sign of weakness or inadequacy is fundamental to the ethos of "Finding Light". This approach offers a space for vulnerability, honesty, and growth by demolishing the widespread notion of stoicism and invincibility commonly associated with youth. Recognising the intrinsic interdependence of mental, emotional, and physical health, it highlights the significance of holistic methods in healing and self-management.

Readers will come across a patchwork of stories in the book, ranging from firsthand recollections of people attempting to make their way through the maze of despair to cutting-edge psychological study findings. Every narrative, thought, and tactic demonstrates the human spirit's tenacity and the transformational potential of compassion. "Finding Light" challenges readers to travel on a path of self-discovery, self-compassion, and self-empowerment via the prism of empathy and understanding.

The handbook provides useful tactics and resources for dealing with depression, overcoming obstacles, and building resilience by drawing on the knowledge of psychologists who specialise in these areas. With everything from therapy methods and mindfulness exercises to advice on building dependable relationships and getting help from a professional, "Finding Light" gives readers a whole arsenal to take back control of their mental health. It also emphasises how crucial it is to de-stigmatize conversations about mental health, promote candid communication, and build supportive and understanding communities.

Fundamentally, "Finding Light" is an ode to the innate tenacity and resiliency of the human spirit—a reminder that even in the most dire circumstances, there is always room for development, change, and rejuvenation. It is a call to action, imploring readers to face their inner shadows and to embrace the light that each and every one of us carries within. This handbook is a steady companion in a world full of obstacles and unknowns, providing comfort, direction, and hope to anybody looking to light the way towards recovery and wholeness.

Let us be mindful as we go out on this trip together that we will inevitably make mistakes, stumble, and experience setbacks in our quest for illumination. However, we are able to endure because of our combined fortitude, unflinching compassion, and shared humanity. May "Finding Light" lead the way towards a day when all young people can access the resources, compassion, and understanding they require to thrive, acting as a light of hope in the shadows.

Chapter 1: understanding youth depression

Depression in young people is a complex problem that goes beyond simple feelings of melancholy or sadness. It is a complicated struggle. It is comprised of a multifaceted interaction of biological, psychological, and environmental elements that have the potential to have a significant impact on the life of a young person. Our journey to understand the complexities of depression in young people begins in this chapter, where we shed light on the prevalence of the condition, the underlying causes of it, and the risk factors that are connected with it.

A Prevalence of Depression in Young People:

According to data, there has been a significant increase in the frequency of depression among young people over the years, which is a grave concern on a global scale. It has been determined by the World Health Organisation (WHO) that depression is one of the most prevalent causes of sickness and impairment among teenagers all over the world. According to studies, roughly ten to twenty percent of teenagers and young adults suffer depression at some point throughout their teenage years. The prevalence of depression varies from region to region and from demographic group to demographic group.

Aspects Contributing to the Risk:

In order to develop successful measures for prevention and intervention, it is essential to have a solid understanding of the underlying causes of depression in young people. Although depression can be caused by a confluence of genetic, biological, and environmental variables, there are some risk factors that make young people more susceptible to developing the condition for the following reasons:

A large increase in the risk of a young person getting depressive symptoms might be attributed to a genetic predisposition. A family history of depression or mental disease can be quite significant.

There are a number of neurobiological factors that contribute to the development of depression. One of these factors is an imbalance in neurotransmitters, such as serotonin and dopamine, which play an important part in the regulation of mood and emotions.

3. Environmental Stressors: Adverse childhood events, trauma, abuse, or neglect can be the cause of depressive symptoms in young people and can also make those

symptoms worse.

4. Pressure from the classroom: High academic expectations and stress related to performance can be overwhelming for young people, which can lead to feelings of inadequacy and despair.

5. Influences from Society: Peer pressure, social isolation, and bullying are all factors that can lead to feelings of loneliness and low self-worth, which can exacerbate the symptoms of psychological depression.

6. Cultural Factors: The cultural norms and expectations that surround mental health may deter young people from seeking help or openly expressing their emotions, which in turn perpetuates stigma and creates barriers to treatment.

Signs and symptoms of depression in young people:

It can be difficult to recognise and treat depression in young people since it frequently manifests itself in a manner that is distinct from that of elderly individuals. Despite the fact that feelings of melancholy and hopelessness are rather widespread, young people may also exhibit subtle signs and symptoms, such as the following:

1. **irritation and hostility**: Instead of displaying overt signs of melancholy, depressed young people may exhibit increased irritation, impatience, or hostility towards other people.
2. **Alterations in Behaviour**: Withdrawal from social activities, changes in sleep patterns, disruptions in eating, and a loss in scholastic performance are all prominent behavioural indications of depression in young people.
3. **Dangerous Behaviour**: As a maladaptive method of coping with emotional discomfort, some young people may engage in risky behaviours, such as abusing substances, inflicting harm on themselves, or driving recklessly.

The Influence of Societal and Cultural Groups:

A number of societal and cultural elements that have an impact on the experiences that young people have in their lives contribute to the incidence of depression among young people.

Stress and anxiety among young people can be made worse by the relentless pursuit of academic performance and competitiveness in educational environments. This can contribute to the development of depression in young people.
2. The effect of Social Media: The pervasive effect of social

media platforms can intensify emotions of inadequacy, comparison, and FOMO (fear of missing out), which can have a negative impact on the self-esteem and mental well-being of young people.

3. The Problem of Stigma in Relation to Mental Health

Despite the fact that awareness is expanding, stigma and misconceptions regarding mental health continue to exist, which prevents young people from seeking assistance and support when they are in need of it.

Change that is Empowering:

Education and awareness are significant weapons that can be used to battle depression in young people and to develop an environment within the community that is supportive:

1. **Early Recognition and Intervention:** We can assist early identification and intervention by teaching parents, educators, and carers about the signs and symptoms of depression in young people. This will help to minimise the impact that depression has on the lives of young people.

The promotion of open discussion helps young people to seek treatment and support without the worry of being judged or feeling ashamed. This is accomplished by creating safe spaces for open communication and by removing the stigma associated with conversations about mental health.

3. Developing Resilience Through: Youth who are provided with the ability to effectively traverse the obstacles that life presents and to recover from adversity are empowered when they are equipped with coping skills, emotional intelligence, and techniques that promote resilience.

4. Efforts Made in Collaboration: It is vital for healthcare professionals, educators, legislators, and community stakeholders to work together in order to adopt holistic ways to combat depression in young people and to promote mental well-being.

In conclusion, depression in young people is a complex problem that calls for an in-depth comprehension of its origins, manifestations, and the ways in which those manifestations are influenced by society. Through the cultivation of empathy, awareness, and proactive action, we have the ability to establish a community that is more empathetic and supportive, encouraging young people to feel empowered to seek assistance, heal, and prosper. In order to prepare the path for a more positive and mentally healthy future, let us work together to shatter the silence that surrounds depression in young people

Chapter 2: Signs and Symptoms

For the purpose of providing early intervention and support, it is crucial to recognise the signs and symptoms of depression in young people. In this chapter, we explore deeper into the different ways that depression can present in young people, covering both common and often ignored signs of the condition.

Depression can exhibit itself in a variety of ways, including changes in appetite or weight, sleep difficulties, and a loss of interest in things that were previously enjoyed. Depression does not always present itself as constant melancholy. Furthermore, adolescents may have physical symptoms such as headaches or stomachaches without any underlying medical cause. These symptoms may be caused by a combination of factors.

In addition, emotional symptoms such as impatience, rage, or feelings of worthlessness may manifest themselves, which frequently results in issues in interpersonal interactions as well as academic achievement. Being watchful and attentive to these behavioural changes is of the utmost importance for parents, teachers, and peers, as they may indicate that the individual is experiencing underlying emotional discomfort.

In addition, teenagers may engage in self-destructive behaviours as a means of coping with the feelings of inner turmoil that they are experiencing. These behaviours may include substance misuse, self-harm, or irresponsible behaviour. It is possible that these acts will temporarily divert them from their anguish; however, in the long run, they will only help to make their emotional misery and feelings of isolation worse.

By being more familiar with the various expressions of depression in young people, we can create an environment that is more helpful and nurturing for adolescents, allowing them to seek treatment without suffering from the fear of being judged or stigmatised. We have the ability to bridge the gap between those who suffer in silence and those who receive the aid and understanding they so sorely require just by engaging in open communication and attentive listening.

Physical Symptoms:

Depression in young people frequently presents itself in the form of physical symptoms that are not directly connected to the emotional suffering that they are experiencing. These can include changes in appetite or weight, where a young person may experience either an increase or decrease in their appetite, leading to apparent changes in weight. These changes can also involve changes in weight. It is also common for adolescents to experience sleep difficulties, with the majority of them either sleeping too much or not sleeping enough. Furthermore, complaints of headaches or stomachaches that do not appear to have any apparent medical causes can be an indication of feelings of emotional distress that are underlying.

Psychological Signs and Symptoms:

Despite the fact that persistent melancholy is one of the most prominent signs of depression, adolescents may also exhibit a wide range of other emotional symptoms in addition to sorrow. There are a number of frequent signs, including irritability, mood swings, rage, and a pervading feeling of worthlessness. It is possible for these emotional changes to have a considerable impact on their day-to-day functioning, which can result in difficulties in both their personal relationships and their academic achievement. When it comes to providing adequate support and resources, it is crucial for carers and educators to pay attention to these emotional changes and provide suitable assistance.

Behaviours that are destructive to oneself:

It is possible for adolescents to engage in self-destructive behaviours as a means of managing their feelings in order to cope with the internal challenges they are experiencing. Addiction to substances, self-inflicted damage, and participation in risky activities are all examples of these behaviours. In spite of the fact that these acts could provide momentary reprieve from emotional suffering, they frequently make the underlying problems even worse and might result in additional feelings of loneliness and distress. In order to safeguard the young person's safety and well-being, it is essential for parents, teachers, and peers to remain watchful for indicators of self-destructive behaviour and to act as soon as possible.

In order to create an environment that is supportive:

The establishment of a supportive and loving environment in which teenagers feel at ease seeking assistance is absolutely necessary in order to properly address the issue of depression in young people. In order to accomplish this, it is necessary to cultivate open communication channels in which young people can feel secure expressing their feelings without the fear of being judged or stigmatised. When it comes to understanding and validating their experiences, active listening and empathy play key roles. This helps to bridge the gap between those who suffer in silence and those who receive the aid they require. We can encourage young people to seek treatment and embark on a road towards healing and recovery if we remove the stigma associated with mental health concerns and promote understanding and acceptance of those who struggle with emotional health.

Conclusion:

In conclusion, it is essential to recognise the signs and symptoms of depression in young people in order to provide help and intervention at an earlier stage. When we have a better awareness of the various ways in which depression can show in young people, including physical symptoms, emotional shifts, and behaviours that are detrimental to themselves, we are better able to provide support and guidance to these kids as they are working towards healing and recovery. In order to break down barriers that prevent teenagers from seeking help and to promote mental well-being among adolescents, it is vital to create an environment that is kind and supportive, where open communication and empathy are valued. Following this, we will look into successful ways for prevention, intervention, and recovery of depression in young people, as well as investigate the numerous factors that contribute to the development of depression in young people. Let us collaborate in order to construct a future in which young people are able to flourish both emotionally and mentally.

Chapter 3: The Impact of Social Media

It is impossible to overstate the impact that social media has had on the lives of young people in today's society, which is more interconnected. The manner in which people communicate, engage, and see both themselves and others has been altered as a result of this. The extensive presence of social media brings forth a plethora of issues, particularly with regard to mental health and well-being, despite the fact that it offers a multitude of advantages.

Comparison is the phenomenon that lies at the centre of this troublesome situation. Social media platforms provide views into the lives of people that have been meticulously curated, and they frequently showcase idealised versions of reality while doing so. Whether it's pictures of beautiful selfies, pictures of exotic holidays, or pictures of accomplishments, these depictions have the potential to set expectations that are not realistic and to foster feelings of inadequacy among older people. Exposure to such stuff on a consistent basis might result in a mistaken perception of oneself as well as an unrelenting desire of perfection that is unreachable.

The digital domain is not immune to the more negative aspects of human behaviour, which is another point to consider. Victims of cyberbullying and online harassment are left feeling lonely and vulnerable as a result of the shockingly widespread prevalence of these behaviours. Because of the anonymity that the internet provides, individuals are emboldened to participate in harmful behaviour without fear of immediate consequences, which amplifies the psychological impact on those who are targeted. Young people are more likely to experience emotions of loneliness, anxiety, and despair as a result of these kinds of situations, which can have a significant impact on their mental health.

All of these problems are made even more complicated by the addictive quality of social media. It is possible to hijack attention and disturb healthy sleep habits by scrolling through feeds, notifications, and likes for an extended period of time. This can result in extreme exhaustion and increased levels of stress. The fear of missing out (FOMO) is a phenomenon that causes people to check their electronic gadgets on a regular basis, which in turn perpetuates a loop of anxiety and compulsion. Because of this, young people are finding themselves increasingly glued to their screens, and as a result, they are giving up meaningful connections and experiences that take place in the real world.

In addition, the increasing incidence of "doomscrolling" adds even another layer of intricacy to the interaction between social media and mental health. Constantly being exposed to upsetting news and information that is negative might contribute to the development of a sense of hopelessness and despair. Whether it be personal tragedies, political turmoil, or global catastrophes, the never-ending stream of negativity can have a detrimental effect on one's emotional well-being, particularly for young people who are susceptible to being influenced by their surroundings.

In order to effectively address these concerns, it is absolutely necessary to foster digital literacy and mindfulness among members of the younger generation. We give them the ability to traverse the digital landscape with better resilience and discernment by providing them with the tools necessary to critically analyse content found online and to recognise the potential impact of that content. In order to offset the negative impact that technology can have on mental health, it is helpful to encourage mindful technology use. This can be accomplished by establishing boundaries about screen time and taking regular breaks from social media.

In addition, it is essential to cultivate offline interactions that are supportive in order to combat the isolating impacts that social media can have. The promotion of face-to-face interactions and meaningful conversations helps to establish social relationships and creates a sense of belonging that cannot be recreated through the use of information technology. Outside of the sphere of digital technology, opportunities for self-expression and fulfilment can be found by participating in activities that foster genuine connection, such as hobbies, sports, or volunteer work.

Furthermore, it is of the utmost importance to utilise technology itself as a tool for the purpose of promoting mental wellness. Those who are battling with mental health concerns can benefit from the resources and assistance that can be provided via the utilisation of online platforms. The particular issues that today's adolescents are confronted with can be addressed through the use of technology, which provides creative solutions such as online therapy sessions and mental health apps.

In the following chapters, we will go deeper into ways for developing healthy behaviours around screen usage, fostering meaningful connections, and utilising technology for the purpose of enhancing mental wellness. We have the ability to enable young people to create a healthy relationship with the digital world and to prioritise their well-being above all else by taking a holistic strategy that addresses the numerous facets of the influence that social media has on mental health.

Chapter 4: Navigating School and Academic Pressure

The educational environment is a crucial arena in the lives of young people, not only for the purpose of achieving academic success but also for the purpose of maintaining mental and emotional equilibrium. Nevertheless, the pervasive culture of academic competitiveness frequently exacts a toll on students, manifesting as stress, anxiety, and even despair in some cases.

Students find themselves engaged in a culture that places a high value on performance and achievement from the very beginning of their educational experience, even if it means being at the expense of their overall health and happiness. They may experience chronic stress and burnout as a result of the dread of failing, which, when combined with the pressure to fulfil expectations, can cast a shadow over their educational path.

Furthermore, the prominence of standardised testing and the unrelenting pursuit of prominent academic institutions both contribute to the intensification of this environment that represents a pressure cooker. In the process of coping with the weight of their future possibilities, students frequently ignore their own self-care and mental health, which contributes to a cycle of stress and tiredness that they continue to perpetuate.

The transition to studying through distant means during the COVID-19 epidemic made these difficulties even more difficult to manage. The students found themselves in a state of isolation, being deprived of the social connections and support networks that were essential for their emotional growth. The consequent emotions of isolation and disconnection enhanced the stressors that were already there, which in turn increased the likelihood of depression, particularly among demographic groups who are more susceptible to the condition.

In order to mitigate the negative impact that academic pressure has on the mental health of young people, it is of the utmost importance to establish an educational environment that is supportive and places an emphasis on overall well-being. The importance of collaboration between educators, parents, and politicians cannot be overstated when it comes to the development of a culture that embraces self-compassion, resilience, and balance.

Additionally, it is of the utmost importance for educational institutions to make available resources and support services related to mental health problems. By removing the stigma associated with mental health concerns and making sure that counselling and other forms of intervention are easily accessible, schools have the ability to cultivate an atmosphere that is friendly to emotional flourishing. When working towards the realisation of this vision, it is absolutely necessary to acknowledge the complex nature of the well-being of students. In the quest of academic brilliance, mental health should not be neglected, nor should academic success be prioritised over mental health. Both of these things should be avoided at all costs.

Through the promotion of open discourse around mental health, one of the most important aspects of creating a supportive school climate is accomplished. It is possible for schools to reduce the stigma associated with mental health issues and empower students to make their own well-being a priority by simply encouraging conversations about emotions, stress management, and getting assistance when it is required.

Additionally, the incorporation of self-care and mindfulness practices into the curriculum can provide students with practical tools that can be utilised for the management of stress and the maintenance of equilibrium. Schools have the ability to give students with actionable skills for fostering resilience and self-compassion. These tactics can be provided in a variety of ways, including special wellness workshops, mindfulness exercises, and the incorporation of relaxation techniques into regular routines.

Furthermore, programmes that are designed to establish social relationships and build a sense of community inside schools have the potential to play a significant role in improving the well-being of students can be of great consequence. The implementation of peer support programmes, the organisation of extracurricular activities with the goal of building positive connections, and the creation of safe places in which students feel valued and accepted are all examples of what might be included in this category.

Beyond the confines of the school environment, it is necessary to work together with parents and other carers in order to assist the mental health of children. Schools have the ability to form a unified front in the promotion of holistic well-being and to ensure that pupils receive continuous assistance both at home and at school if they involve parents in discussions regarding academic pressure and mental health.

Additionally, cooperation with specialists in the field of mental health and community organisations have the potential to expand the social support system that is accessible to students. It is possible for schools to guarantee that children have access to the complete care they require in order to flourish by establishing connections between students and external resources such as counselling services, support groups, and mental health hotlines.

In conclusion, in order to successfully navigate the challenge of school and academic pressure, it is necessary for all parties involved in the education system to make a concerted effort. Enabling children to achieve academic success while simultaneously promoting their emotional well-being can be accomplished by placing an emphasis on mental health, encouraging kids to develop resilience, and establishing a school atmosphere that is helpful.

In the following chapters, we will delve deeper into particular strategies and interventions for increasing student well-being in the context of academic pressure. These will be discussed individually and collectively. Together, let us continue to work for an education system that takes a holistic approach, one that acknowledges the inherent relationship that exists between academic achievement and mental health, and one that places a priority on the overall well-being of each and every student.

Chapter 5: Family Dynamics and Support Systems

The dynamics within our families are analogous to the unseen threads that are woven into the fabric of our lives. They are responsible for moulding our identities, influencing our behaviours, and having a significant impact on our mental and emotional well-being. When it comes to young people, the family unit acts as a crucible in which they learn to negotiate the complexities of relationships, emotions, and the process of discovering who they are a person. In this chapter, we dig into the complex relationship that exists between the dynamics of the family and the occurrence of depression in young people. We draw attention to the essential role that supportive relationships and communication play in the development of resilience and well-being.

The Crucial Role of Family Support:

The presence of a familial environment that is both supportive and nurturing is essential to the development of a resilient young person. Families are the major source of emotional nutrition, not only because they offer a safe harbour in the midst of the storms of life, but also because they provide a foundation of unconditional love and acceptance. Families are able to establish an environment in which teenagers feel seen, heard, and appreciated when they encourage open communication, active listening, and empathy among their adult children. Both resilience and self-esteem are strengthened as a result of this sense of belonging and connection, which acts as a buffer against the challenges that come with puberty.

On the other hand, families that are characterised by conflict, emotional neglect, or dysfunction can become breeding grounds for sadness and despair. It is possible for young people to internalise their challenges when communication breaks down and emotions are repressed or dismissed. This can result in feelings of loneliness, isolation, and inadequacy. Consequently, the cultivation of healthy family dynamics is not only a matter of convenience; rather, it is an essential requirement for the protection of the mental health of young people.

Finding Your Way Through the Expectations and Conflicts of Your Family:

Expectations, tensions, and rivalries have the potential to become significant sources of stress for young people, and they frequently originate within the complicated fabric of family life. Inadequate and self-doubting feelings can be fueled by the enormous amount of pressure that is exerted on adolescents by their parents' expectations, whether those expectations are explicit or tacit. Furthermore, sibling rivalry and disputes between generations can also contribute to the development of tension within the family unit, which in turn can exacerbate mental suffering.

It is necessary for families to build an atmosphere of empathy, understanding, and mutual respect in order to reduce the impact of familial demands and conflicts on the levels of depression experienced by young people. In order to accomplish this, it is necessary to encourage open communication, to establish expectations that are attainable, and to recognise the particular capabilities and constraints of each individual. Through the cultivation of a culture of acceptance and support, families have the ability to encourage young people to embrace their identities in an authentic manner and to negotiate the obstacles that they face within their families with fortitude and grace.

Regarding the Elimination of Stigma and the Encouragement of Help-Seeking Behaviour:

The stigma, shame, and myths that surround mental health continue to be prevalent barriers that prevent people from seeking treatment in many different cultures. It is possible for adolescents who are struggling with depression to be hindered in their capacity to disclose their issues or seek professional support because they fear that their relatives will judge them or reject them. In light of this, it is the responsibility of families to combat stigma, increase mental health awareness, and establish an environment that is free of judgement and encourages and normalises conversations about feelings and well-being.

Destroying the stigma that is associated with depression and empowering young people to prioritise their mental health can be accomplished by families through the cultivation of an atmosphere that is characterised by trust and open communication. In order to accomplish this, it may be necessary to educate family members on the signs and symptoms of depression, to remove the stigma associated with treatment and medication, and to demonstrate good coping techniques for managing stress and emotions. Family members have the potential to play a vital role in supporting early intervention and rehabilitation for teenagers who are battling with depression. This can be accomplished through collaborative efforts to promote help-seeking behaviour.

Facilitating the Development of Resilience and Connection:

The cultivation of a sense of belonging and connection within the family unit is ultimately the most important factor in the development of resilience in young people. In situations where adolescents see that their families are providing them with support, value, and understanding, they are better ready to face the obstacles that life presents with self-assurance and optimism. Through the cultivation of constructive relationships, the promotion of healthy communication, and the demonstration of perseverance in the face of hardship, families have the potential to serve as pillars of strength and support for the subsequent generation.

In conclusion, the dynamics of the family have a significant influence in the formation of the mental and emotional well-being of young people. Creating a loving environment that supports teenagers to thrive can be accomplished by families through the cultivation of supportive relationships, the resolution of conflicts, the combating of stigma, and the promotion of behaviour that encourages seeking assistance. Building stronger, healthier families that will serve as a source of hope and healing for future generations is something that can be accomplished via communal efforts to foster resilience and connectedness.

Chapter 6: Coping Mechanisms and Self-Care Practices

The toolset for managing the symptoms of depression and supporting overall well-being should include coping techniques and self-care routines. This is especially true during the turbulent years of adolescence, when the symptoms of depression are particularly difficult to manage. The purpose of this chapter is to provide teenagers with the means to deal with stress, control their emotions, and nurture resilience in the face of adversity. This chapter addresses a wide range of strategies and procedures that are aimed to accomplish these goals.

Healthy Coping Skills

Developing healthy coping abilities is one of the most important aspects of efficient coping, and it is also highly recommended. The acquisition of problem-solving tactics, techniques for mood management, and assertive communication can be of tremendous assistance to adolescents. We empower children to negotiate the obstacles of life with greater efficacy by teaching them to identify their emotions, question harmful thought patterns, and express themselves in a constructive manner. This ultimately results in the development of emotional resilience.

Reduction of Stress and Relaxation from Stress

Participating in activities that are targeted towards relaxation and stress reduction can be of tremendous benefit to adolescents who are struggling with negative emotions such as anxiety and depression. An awareness and acceptance of the present moment can be fostered via the practice of mindfulness, meditation, and deep breathing exercises. These practices help to reduce rumination and cultivate a sense of serenity and inner peace in the midst of the chaos that is human life.

Practices that promote a healthy lifestyle

When it comes to sustaining one's entire well-being and mental health, maintaining a healthy lifestyle is of the utmost importance. Exercising on a consistent basis, maintaining healthy eating habits, and getting enough sleep are all important pillars in this regard. In instance, engaging in physical exercise causes the release of endorphins, which are neurotransmitters that are responsible for promoting sensations of happiness and bliss. Additionally, maintaining good nutrition and sleep hygiene provide the body and mind with the critical resources that are necessary for optimal functioning.

Support Groups for Social Interactions

In order for teenagers to successfully navigate the intricacies of mental health difficulties, it is essential to cultivate powerful social support networks. Building relationships with people you know, including friends, family, and adults you can rely on, can provide you with a sense of belonging, validation, and emotional support while you are going through a difficult period. In order to alleviate feelings of loneliness and isolation, it is beneficial to engage in constructive social contacts and seek assistance from reliable others. This, in turn, helps to reduce the likelihood of developing depression and strengthens emotional resilience.

Empowerment and self-efficacy are two concepts.

One of the most important things that can be done to empower teenagers to take an active role in their mental health and well-being is to encourage them to engage in self-care routines and coping skills. The cultivation of a feeling of agency and self-efficacy, which enables individuals to face the challenges that life throws at them with perseverance and fortitude, can be accomplished by providing them with the necessary knowledge, skills, and resources.

Conclusion

Following this, we will go into specific coping methods and self-care practices that teenagers can incorporate into their everyday life to improve mental wellness and resilience. These practices and tactics can be found in the following chapters. Let us work together to provide young people with the tools and resources they require to navigate the turbulent terrain of adolescence with the fortitude, courage, and resilience they need to succeed. Through the cultivation of their coping strategies and practices of self-care, we are laying the groundwork for a future in which teenagers flourish, armed with the resilience to weather the storms of life and emerge stronger on the other side.

Chapter 7: Seeking Professional Help: Therapy and Counseling

Seeking the assistance of a trained professional becomes a ray of light in the midst of the darkness that is experienced during the journey through the depths of depression. It is possible that personal coping methods and self-care routines, despite the fact that they provide significant assistance, are not sufficient for those who are struggling with severe or persistent symptoms. Within the scope of this chapter, we investigate the essential role that therapy and counselling play in reducing depression in young people, as well as the various therapeutic treatments that are adapted to meet the specific requirements of adolescents.

The purpose of therapy is to provide teenagers with a safe space in which they can untangle the tangled web of their ideas, feelings, and experiences in a setting that is both confidential and compassionate. They begin a journey of self-discovery here, with the assistance of a qualified therapist, with the goal of determining the causes of their depression and developing coping skills and resilience in the process.

Cognitive-Behavioral Therapy (often known as CBT) says:

Cognitive-Behavioral Therapy (CBT), a guiding light of evidence-based treatment that is well-known for its effectiveness in treating depression in adolescents, is at the forefront of therapeutic interventions. The cognitive behavioural therapy (CBT) approach is based on the idea that our ideas, feelings, and behaviours are all interconnected and have a significant impact on our mental health overall. The cognitive behavioural therapy (CBT) programme teaches teenagers how to recognise and challenge harmful thought patterns, thereby replacing them with alternatives that are more productive. Through the process of disentangling the complex web of mistaken perceptions, they are able to acquire a greater sense of clarity and agency, which enables them to handle the challenges that life presents with resiliency and optimism.

Interpersonal Therapy (also known as IPT):
Relationships are an essential component in the complex tapestry that is the life of adolescents, as they have a significant role in determining their emotional environment. The field of interpersonal therapy, often known as IPT, has emerged as a ray of light, shedding light on the way to recovery by examining the dynamics of interpersonal

relationships. The goal of interpersonal performance therapy (IPT) is to improve communication skills, cultivate healthy boundaries, and resolve problems between individuals. Through the cultivation of meaningful connections and the strengthening of their support networks, adolescents are able to navigate the turbulent terrain of depression with a newly discovered sense of strength and unity.

The acronym "Dialectical Behaviour Therapy" means "DBT."

The Dialectical Behaviour Therapy (DBT) programme provides a haven of peace and self-empowerment for teenagers who are struggling with overwhelming feelings and tumultuous inner storms. By combining aspects of cognitive behavioural therapy (CBT) with mindfulness practices, dialectical behaviour therapy (DBT) provides teenagers with the abilities necessary to control their feelings, develop a tolerance for suffering, and traverse challenges of interpersonal relationships with grace and resilience. A transforming path of self-discovery is embarked upon by adolescents through dialectical behaviour therapy (DBT), and they emerge from the crucible of hardship with newly discovered wisdom and inner peace.

*

Finding the Right Therapist:

When navigating the complex landscape of mental health treatment, one of the most important steps on the road to recovery is locating the appropriate therapist. Encouragement is given to adolescents to seek out therapists who are trained to work with young people and who are equipped with the knowledge and compassion necessary to handle the specific requirements of adolescents. The foundation of successful therapy is the development of a trustworthy and cooperative relationship between the client and the therapist. This creates a secure environment in which the client can engage in self-exploration, personal development, and healing.

Breaking the Stigma: In the effort to remove the stigma associated with mental health care, adolescents play a crucial role as the torchbearers of change. By bravely seeking assistance and sharing their experiences, individuals are challenging the widespread beliefs and prejudices that are associated with depression. This helps to pave the way for a society that is more sympathetic and welcoming to those who are different. It is possible for us to eliminate the obstacles that prevent adolescents from gaining access to mental health treatment by means of collective action and advocacy. This will guarantee that every adolescent is provided with the necessary support and help to fully develop.Discovering

Your Way Through the Therapeutic Process:
When adolescents begin their journey through therapy, they are confronted with a landscape that is rife with obstacles and victories, failures and breakthroughs. They are guided by the unshakable support of their therapist and the resiliency of their spirit as they take each step forward in the process of confronting the shadows of their past and the uncertainties of their future. As they make their way along this twisting road, they excavate hidden emotions, confront old beliefs, and cultivate novel insights. As a result, they emerge from the furnace of therapy with renewed clarity and purpose.

Recognising and Overcoming Obstacles to Treatment:
In spite of the fact that therapy holds a great deal of promise, adolescents frequently face significant obstacles on their path to treatment. The challenges that they face, which range from financial restraints to cultural stigmas, are significant and have the potential to jeopardise their progress towards healing. Despite this, teenagers are able to overcome these obstacles by relying upon the resources of their communities, support networks, and advocacy activities in order to gain access to the care that they are entitled to receive. By increasing awareness and promoting collaboration, we can eliminate the obstacles that prevent adolescents from gaining access to mental health care. This will ensure that no

adolescent is left to navigate the maze of depression on their own.

Facilitating the Development of Resilience and Well-Being: The quest of resilience and well-being, which serves as a beacon of hope in the midst of the storms of depression, is at the core of the therapeutic journey. With the help of the transforming force of therapy, teenagers are able to grow the inner strength and resilience necessary to weather the challenges that life throws at them. As a result, they emerge from the furnace of depression with a newfound wisdom and resilience. By embracing self-care routines, cultivating meaningful connections, and cultivating a sense of purpose, teenagers are able to construct a path towards long-term well-being, recovering their lives from the grip of despair, and embracing a future that is full with hope and opportunity.

Conclusion:

There is a story of resiliency, healing, and optimism that is woven into the fabric of adolescent life through the threads of therapy and counselling relationships. When teenagers are exposed to the transforming power of therapy, they begin on a journey of self-discovery, during which they confront the shadows of their past and embrace the promise of a better tomorrow. They are able to traverse the maze of sadness with resiliency and resolve, and they emerge from the furnace of treatment with a greater sense of purpose, clarity, and resilience. Let us work together to eliminate the stigma that is associated with mental health treatment, provide young people the ability to seek the assistance they require, and create a future in which every young person has the opportunity to flourish.

Chapter 8: Medication and Alternative Treatments

Medication and alternative therapies are two important pathways that can be utilised in the complex landscape of treating depression in adolescents. These therapies have the potential to manage symptoms and promote mental well-being. It is essential for teenagers, their families, and healthcare providers alike to have a solid understanding of the roles, benefits, and considerations associated with these specific techniques.

Medication, particularly antidepressants such as selective serotonin reuptake inhibitors (SSRIs) and serotonin and norepinephrine reuptake inhibitors (SNRIs), is an essential component of pharmacological therapies for the treatment of depression in young people. These drugs are able to successfully treat symptoms and restore emotional equilibrium because they target chemical imbalances in the brain. The utilisation of these substances, on the other hand, calls for close monitoring and the participation of medical professionals in order to determine the most appropriate dosage and minimise the risk of adverse effects. Importantly, medication is frequently used into a more comprehensive treatment framework that also includes mental health counselling or therapy. This highlights the significance of taking a holistic approach to the treatment of mental health issues in adolescents.

The use of alternative and complementary treatments provides other possibilities for the treatment of depression in adolescents. These therapies supplement conventional treatment modalities with a variety of alternative approaches that are aimed at achieving holistic well-being.

It has been found that exercise is an effective method for treating depression because it makes use of the mood-enhancing benefits that are associated with physical activity. Exercise acts as a natural antidepressant because it causes the production of endorphins, which in turn promotes emotions of happiness and vigour. In addition to fostering emotional resilience and psychological well-being, encouraging teenagers to participate in regular physical activity not only improves their physical health but also promotes their physical health.

Mood management can be aided by nutritional supplements, which include vital vitamins and minerals such as omega-3 fatty acids, vitamin D, and folate. These supplements may also be used in conjunction with pharmacological therapies.

Including these supplements in an adolescent's diet can improve their overall mental health and potentially alleviate symptoms of depression, despite the fact that they are not a treatment in and of themselves.

Yoga, tai chi, and acupuncture are examples of mind-body activities that offer holistic approaches to the therapy of depression. These practices place an emphasis on the concept that the mind, body, and spirit are all interconnected. Teenagers are equipped with vital tools for navigating the intricacies of their mental health journey when they engage in these practices, which develop relaxation, stress reduction, and emotional balance.

In addition to providing teenagers with a creative channel through which they can express and process their feelings, art therapy also provides a nonverbal medium through which they can explore themselves and find healing. Self-expression, catharsis, and empowerment are all fostered by the participation in artistic endeavours such as painting, drawing, or the creation of music. This enables teenagers to use their intrinsic creativity as a vehicle for emotional resilience.

Through the cultivation of present-moment awareness and emotional control, the practices of mindfulness and meditation provide teenagers with vital tools for navigating the problems that are associated with depression. Rumination is reduced and inner calm is cultivated via the practice of mindfulness, which also helps to promote resilience in the face of hardship. Mindfulness techniques build acceptance, nonjudgment, and self-compassion.

In order to successfully navigate the therapeutic landscape for adolescent depression, it is absolutely necessary for adolescents and their families to adopt a holistic strategy that incorporates medication, therapy, and alternative treatments. The potential for recovery and long-term mental health for teenagers can be maximised through the utilisation of synergies between the various modalities that are available to them.

In order to develop resilience and facilitate recovery, it is of the utmost importance to provide teenagers with the ability to investigate a variety of treatment alternatives and to advocate for their own requirements and preferences. It is possible to develop a supportive atmosphere that is conducive to holistic growth and thriving if we foster a collaborative collaboration between adolescents, their families, and healthcare practitioners.

In the next chapters, we will look more into the various ways that can be utilised to incorporate medicine, therapy, and other treatments into a comprehensive treatment plan for depression in young people. As we traverse the complexity of adolescent mental health and work towards a future of healing and well-being, let us embark together on a journey of discovery, resilience, and empowerment. Let us do this together.

Chapter 9: Overcoming Stigma and Seeking Help

Introduction

Even though stigma and misunderstandings about mental health continue to exist in today's culture, youth depression continues to be a widespread problem. These factors continue to operate as significant obstacles that prevent individuals from seeking assistance and receiving the necessary therapy. We delve into the deep influence that stigma has on teenagers who are struggling with depression in this chapter. We also investigate successful techniques for overcoming these obstacles in order to encourage students to seek help and to cultivate a culture that is accepting and supportive of those who are struggling with depression.

Having an Understanding of Stigma

Stigma is characterised by unfavourable attitudes, beliefs, and stereotypes that are associated with mental illness. This stigma can result in discrimination, social exclusion, and a widespread reluctance to seek assistance. Internalised stigma is a common problem for adolescents who are experiencing depression. These adolescents may struggle with emotions of shame or embarrassment over their disease, in addition to the outward stigma that they face from their peers, family members, or society as a whole.

Promoting Awareness and Education as a Means of Combating Stigma

Education and awareness are becoming more effective instruments in the fight against stigma. By providing factual information about depression, challenging misconceptions, and cultivating empathy and understanding, we may reduce the stigma associated with depression and develop an environment that is more helpful and inclusive for adolescents who are navigating mental health problems.

Personal tales are an essential component in humanising depression and working to dispel misconceptions about the condition. Through the sharing of their own personal experiences, teenagers are given the ability to speak honestly about the challenges they face, which helps to cultivate an environment in which requesting support is met with empathy rather than judgement. The journey towards mental wellbeing is made easier for adolescents by the presence of peer support groups and online forums, which provide essential resources and a sense of community.

Considering the Integration of Mental Health Education

Education regarding mental health should be incorporated into the curriculum of schools; this is an essential step towards normalising conversations about mental illness. The stigma that is associated with mental health can be considerably reduced and teenagers can be empowered to seek treatment when they are in need of it if schools encourage open discourse and provide students with the knowledge and tools necessary to understand and address their own mental health.

Involving Parents, Caregivers, and Trusted Adults

When it comes to establishing a network of support for teenagers who are battling with depression, the function that parents, carers, and other adults who can be trusted plays a significant role. The promotion of open communication, active listening, and the validating of feelings helps to cultivate an atmosphere of safety and acceptance, which in turn reduces the fear of stigma and encourages individuals to seek assistance.

Empowering Adolescents

It is of the utmost importance to provide these young people with the understanding that they are not alone and that assistance is available to them. We are able to instill hope and resilience in teenagers who are struggling with mental illness if we shatter the silence that surrounds depression in young people and cultivate a culture of acceptance and support.

Conclusion

For the purpose of reducing stigma and encouraging help-seeking behaviour among teenagers who are experiencing depression, it is necessary for a variety of stakeholders to collaborate in order to achieve these goals. If we make education a top priority, encourage open communication, and cultivate surroundings that are supportive, we will be able to eliminate the obstacles that prevent teenagers from receiving mental health care and ensure that they are provided with the resources and support they require to flourish. As a group, let us work towards the establishment of a society that appreciates, comprehends, and places a high priority on the mental health of every single person.

Chapter 10: Building Resilience and Emotional Strength

Resilience is not simply the ability to recover from misfortune; rather, it is the capacity to adjust, develop, and flourish in spite of the difficulties that life presents. In the case of adolescents, this resilience serves as an essential defence mechanism against depression and other mental health problems. The purpose of this chapter is to look into tactics that are geared at giving teenagers the tools they need to traverse the difficulties of life with fortitude and optimism. These strategies are designed to foster resilience and emotional strength in adolescents.

Developing a growth mindset is one of the most important aspects of resilience. In this way of thinking, failures are reframed as chances for personal development and improvement. For adolescents who adopt this point of view, they are better able to persevere through challenges and to keep hope for the future, even when confronted with hardship.

In addition, it is of the utmost importance to cultivate both self-awareness and emotional intelligence. We give teenagers the ability to face the challenges of life with self-assurance and resiliency by assisting them in recognising and managing their emotions, gaining an understanding of their capabilities and limitations, and adopting healthy coping techniques.

In addition, providing teenagers with a sense of purpose and meaning in their lives can be an effective way to motivate them when they are going through challenging circumstances. They will develop a sense of direction and resilience, which will contribute to an improvement in their overall well-being, if they are encouraged to pursue their passions, establish objectives, and participate in activities that are in line with their values.

In addition, it is essential to cultivate healthy relationships and social contacts wherever possible. In addition to providing affirmation, encouragement, and emotional sustenance, strong support networks act as a buffer against the negative effects of stress and hardship.

It is essential to create circumstances that are supportive, in addition to individual considerations. The development of resilience is a process that involves the participation of families, communities, and schools. In addition to fostering a sense of belonging and fostering social-emotional learning, they can provide possibilities for personal development and progress.

It is possible to equip teenagers with the ability to overcome challenges and survive in a world that is unpredictable by providing them with the tools of resilience and emotional strength. In the following chapters, we will look into particular techniques and treatments that are targeted at boosting the overall well-being of adolescents by bolstering their resilience. Let's work together to encourage the development of a new generation of individuals who are able to face the challenges that life throws at them with bravery, fortitude, and encouragement.In addition, it is of the utmost importance to acknowledge that the process of developing resilience is an ongoing one that calls for consistently providing support and reinforcement. Teenagers are likely to face a variety of hurdles throughout their trip; therefore, it is of the utmost importance to equip them with the resources and direction they require in order to successfully manage these problems.

Promoting problem-solving skills is an effective technique for promoting resilience in adolescents. This strategy can be used to foster resilience in adolescents. Providing young people with the knowledge and skills necessary to recognise obstacles, break them down into steps that are more manageable, and devise proactive solutions gives them the ability to face adversity with self-assurance and endurance.

Furthermore, it is essential to foster a sense of autonomy and self-efficacy in each individual. It is more likely that adolescents will confront obstacles with drive and resilience if they have the belief that they have the ability to affect the situations in which they find themselves. Fostering a sense of empowerment and resilience in other people can be accomplished by encouraging them to take initiative, make decisions, and accept responsibility for their actions.

In addition, enhancing the resilience of teenagers can be accomplished by providing them with opportunity to participate in activities that encourage mindfulness and stress reduction. They can be equipped with useful tools for managing stress, improving emotional regulation, and building resilience in the face of adversity through the practice of activities such as meditation, yoga, and deep breathing exercises.

Building resilience also involves encouraging healthy risk-taking and tenacity, which is another crucial part of the process. Resilience and a growth mindset can be fostered in teenagers by encouraging them to engage in activities that are outside of their comfort zones, to try new things, and to learn from their mistakes. Developing the self-assurance and resiliency necessary to negotiate the unpredictability of life is something that young people can accomplish by accepting challenges and persevering through mistakes.

Developing a feeling of community and belonging in adolescents is also a key component in the process of establishing resilience in this age group. The cultivation of a sense of belonging and social support, which are essential protective factors against depression and other mental health concerns, can be accomplished by creating environments that are inclusive and in which young people feel valued, supported, and linked to others.

In addition, it is of the utmost importance to address the structural hurdles and disparities that may impede the capacity of adolescents to develop resilience. By fighting for policies and activities that promote fairness, access to resources, and social justice, we may build environments that are more supportive of all young people, so empowering them to thrive and prosper.

In conclusion, the process of developing resiliency and emotional strength in teenagers needs to be approached from a holistic perspective because it involves multiple aspects. It is possible to equip young people with the ability to navigate the challenges of life with resilience, optimism, and hope for the future if we cultivate a growth mindset, promote self-awareness and emotional intelligence, cultivate purpose and meaning, cultivate healthy relationships and social connections, and create environments that are supportive. A generation of resilient individuals who are equipped to face the uncertainties of life with courage and resilience should be cultivated via continued investments in the well-being of adolescents. Let us continue to invest in the well-being of adolescents together.

Chapter 11: Cultivating Healthy Relationships

The geography of connections during adolescence is crucial in determining a person's emotional resiliency and well-being. This chapter explores the significant importance of fostering good relationships and provides advice on how teenagers can build strong bonds with their family, friends, and other helpful people.

The Importance of Healthy Relationships

The foundation of sound relationships is where teenagers develop their emotional resilience. They offer a safe haven of acceptance, affirmation, and emotional support, protecting against the winds of loneliness and depression. Building strong bonds based on respect, trust, and empathy between friends is like creating a safety net that reduces feelings of loneliness and boosts self-esteem.

Interaction: The Link to Understanding

Meaningful connections are nourished by effective communication. Learning communication skills such as assertiveness, active listening, and dispute resolution is very beneficial for adolescents. With the use of these tools, individuals may express their ideas and emotions more honestly, which promotes peace and understanding in their social interactions.

Respect and Well-Being: Fostering Boundaries and Self-Care

Setting limits and taking care of oneself are essential components of a healthy relationship. Setting boundaries and putting their own needs first in relationships helps adolescents avoid burnout and retain their feeling of independence. They promote an atmosphere of respect and cooperation by being adamant about their wants and boundaries.

Looking for Inspiration and Guidance: Mentors' Role

Mentors become guiding lights in the mosaic of teenage development, showing the way through all the bends and turns of life. Adolescents benefit much from the wisdom, perspective, and encouragement that come from being encouraged to look for strong role models and mentors. These mentors turn into resilient role models, enabling teenagers to face obstacles head-on with dignity and resolve.

Family: The Cornerstone of Assistance

An endless source of love and understanding is found within the family's embrace. Family events, customs, and rituals strengthen the relationships that bind relatives and give teenagers a haven of safety amid the uncertainty of life. Creating a stronger sense of family ties fosters a sense of solidarity and belonging that supports mental health.

Self-determination via Interaction

Adolescents who cultivate good relationships are better able to create support networks that help them weather the ups and downs of life. These relationships act as mooring points, stabilizing them during turbulent times and boosting them during successful ones. We plant the seeds of empowerment and resilience in the rich soil of adolescence when we promote the development of healthy relationships.

Investigating Methods for Developing Good Relationships

With this understanding of the critical role that good relationships play in our lives, let's look at some particular tactics that teenagers can use to build strong bonds in a variety of contexts.

1. Relationships with Peers:

Teens should be encouraged to join clubs or group activities that are related to their interests. These mutual interests-based activities offer a great way for people to connect and become friends.

Instruct students in dispute resolution techniques, stressing the value of empathy and compromise. Adolescents can fortify their friendships and develop conflict-resilience by being given the skills necessary to resolve conflicts in a constructive manner.

Encourage kindness and inclusivity. Teens can actively build a culture of acceptance and belonging in their social circles by reaching out to peers who might be feeling alone or alienated.

2. Links with Family:

Establish opportunities for your family to spend quality time together, such frequent dinners or weekend excursions. These common experiences foster close ties within the family and offer a forum for candid dialogue.

Adolescents should be encouraged to thank and show thanks to family members. Saying "thank you" or writing notes of appreciation are small but powerful ways to strengthen emotional bonds and promote mutual respect in the family.

Arrange family get-togethers where everyone can share their opinions and worries. This exercise emphasizes the value of respecting each family member's viewpoint while encouraging active listening and problem-solving abilities.

3. Advisory and Mentoring:

Urge teenagers to look for mentors or role models in their areas of interest or personal growth. Whether via official programs or unofficial connections, mentors can provide priceless advice and assistance on overcoming obstacles in the workplace, in school, or in personal life.

Encourage people to take advantage of networking possibilities by going to conferences, workshops, and local events. Adolescents have access to a range of viewpoints and possible mentors in these settings, who can encourage and mentor them along the way.

Teens should be encouraged to look for mentorship opportunities on their own initiative. Proactive engagement creates meaningful mentorship relationships, whether it is through reaching out to professionals in their field of interest or making connections with older peers who have relevant knowledge to contribute.

Conclusion:

Adolescents can actively create healthy connections that enhance their lives and improve their general well-being by putting these techniques into practice. A fulfilling and resilient adolescence is based on building connections that are based on empathy, respect, and mutual support, whether in peer interactions, family dynamics, or mentorship relationships. Adolescents who choose these practices set off on a path of self-improvement and community, equipped to face obstacles head-on and with poise.

Chapter 12: Discovering Meaning and Purpose

Finding a sense of purpose and meaning in life is essential for the general well-being of teenagers, and it can have a substantial impact on the mental health of these young people. Our discussion in this chapter delves into the significance of locating one's purpose and meaning in life, as well as the methods that may be utilized to aid teens in determining their interests and principles.

Comprehending the Meaning and Purpose of Something
Being connected to something that is bigger than oneself and having the conviction that one's life has some sort of meaning are both necessary components of having a sense of purpose. It has been found that adolescents who have a distinct sense of purpose are more likely to have more resilience when confronted with adversities, experience higher levels of life satisfaction, and have a lower likelihood of having symptoms of depression.

Investigating One's Values, Individual Talents, and Interests encouraging adolescents to investigate their interests, abilities, and values is a method that has proven to be beneficial in assisting them in discovering their purpose in life. Teenagers are able to feel a great sense of fulfillment that is not limited to short setbacks when they participate in activities that are congruent with their principles and resonate with their passions.

Developing a mindset that is both growth-oriented and resilient

Through the cultivation of a growth mentality and a resilience mindset, it is possible to provide teenagers with assistance in overcoming challenges that they encounter on their path to discovering their purpose. It is possible to empower kids to remain resilient and focused on their goals by encouraging them to perceive problems as opportunities for growth, to learn from setbacks, and to continue in the face of adversity.

Participating in acts of selflessness and service

It is also possible to foster a feeling of purpose and fulfillment in adolescents by encouraging their participation in activities that promote activities that promote service and charity. A profound sense of connection and purpose can be cultivated in the lives of adolescents through activities such as volunteering, participating in community service efforts, and doing acts of kindness. These activities not only help an individual but also benefit others.

Making Connections with Mentors Who Are Supportive

It is possible to give adolescents with essential counsel and inspiration by facilitating relationships with supportive mentors and role models who exemplify purposeful life. Mentors provide adolescents with useful guidance, a different point of view, and support, which enables them to pursue their passions and bring about constructive change in the world.

Providing Adolescents with Agency

In order to equip teenagers with the ability to handle the challenges that life presents with perseverance, optimism, and a clear sense of direction, we provide assistance to them in the process of establishing purpose and meaning in their lives. Over the course of the next chapters, we will look into particular tactics and treatments that are geared at assisting adolescents in discovering their purpose and living their lives with intention. In order to encourage and assist young people as they embark on a journey of self-discovery and purposeful living, let us work together to provide them with inspiration and support. --- ---

The significance of purpose and meaning in the lives of adolescents is investigated in this chapter, along with many methods that may be utilized to assist adolescents in identifying their interests and principles. Each strategy is intended to empower adolescents on their journey toward living a life with a purpose, whether it is through the exploration of hobbies or the development of resilience.

Chapter 13: Mindfulness and Meditation Techniques

Young people in today's fast-paced society are confronted with a wide variety of issues that have the potential to have an effect on their mental health. Stress and anxiety can be common during the teenage years due to a variety of factors, including academic pressure and social dynamics. The practices of mindfulness and meditation, on the other hand, are a ray of light that shines through the midst of the disaster. Within the scope of this chapter, we delve into the deep advantages that these practices offer, as well as provide adolescents with actionable ways that they may use to incorporate them into their everyday lives.

Comprehending the Concept of Mindfulness

In its most fundamental form, mindfulness is characterized by the practice of being fully present in the moment, without attachment or judgment. It requires a person to pay attention to their thoughts, feelings, and sensations while maintaining an open mind and a sense of curiosity. The cultivation of mindfulness can be a transforming practice for adolescents, who frequently find themselves feeling overwhelmed by many things, including school, relationships, and their own sense of identity.

The practice of mindful breathing is one of the most straightforward yet effective forms of mindfulness training. Teenagers should be encouraged to sit quietly and concentrate on their breathing for a few minutes before and after school each day. As they take a breath in and out, they are able to examine the feelings that occur within their body, including the rise and fall of their chest as well as the rhythm of their breathing. These practices not only serve to firmly establish things in the here and now, but they also have the effect of calming the mind and lowering levels of stress and worry.

Engaging in the Practice of Mindful Eating

Teaching teenagers to eat thoughtfully can have a significant impact on their relationship with food as well as their general well-being, particularly in a culture that is characterized by the prevalence of fast food and eating while simultaneously distracted. In the practice of mindful eating, one is able to pay attention to the sensory experience of eating and relish each bite without being distracted or judging the experience.

Adolescents should be encouraged to slow down at meals, to put aside their phones and other distractions, and to concentrate entirely on the process of eating. In addition to chewing slowly and thoughtfully, you should encourage them to take note of the colors, textures, and flavors of the food they are eating. Adolescents can develop healthier eating habits and a greater appreciation for the nutrients that food provides if they are encouraged to build a deeper connection to the experience of eating.

Insights into the Power of Meditation

Through the practice of meditation, individuals have been able to build inner serenity, clarity, and compassion for ages. Meditation can be a safe haven for adolescents, who may be struggling to cope with the stress of school and the expectations of society. It is a means to calm the mind and find peace in the middle of the chaos.

Guided meditation practices provide an organized approach to meditation, which can be very beneficial for individuals who are just beginning their meditation journey. One example of this is the practice of body scans, which involves systematically bringing awareness to each region of the body in order to eliminate tension and encourage relaxation. The practice of building feelings of compassion and goodwill toward oneself and others is the primary focus of loving-kindness meditation. On the other hand, gratitude meditation entails contemplating the aspects of one's life for which they are grateful.

Encourage young people to meditate for a short period of time every day, beginning with a short period of time and progressively increasing the amount of time they meditate for as they become more accustomed to the practice. Encourage them to incorporate meditation into their daily routine, whether it be first thing in the morning, before going to bed, or during a break from studying. Consistency is the key because it is the most important thing.

Reducing Stress Through the Practice of Mindfulness

Mindfulness-based stress reduction (MBSR) programs provide program participants with a methodical way to introducing mindfulness into their everyday lives. Mindfulness meditation, yoga, and cognitive-behavioral approaches are some of the practices that are frequently included in these programs. It has been demonstrated that these programs can reduce stress and increase general well-being.

Encourage young people to investigate Mindfulness-Based Stress Reduction (MBSR) programs locally or online. In addition to fostering resilience, these programs teach participants vital skills and strategies for managing stress, regulating emotions, and managing stress. Participants in Mindfulness-Based Stress Reduction (MBSR) programs have the opportunity to cultivate a more profound understanding of oneself and acquire useful techniques that can help them navigate the challenges of life with greater ease and equanimity.

Providing Adolescents with Agency
By incorporating mindfulness and meditation techniques into their daily lives, adolescents can be given the ability to create greater resilience, emotional balance, and overall well-being. Being able to handle the ups and downs of adolescence with clarity and grace is something that may be accomplished by learning to be fully present in each moment. It is our responsibility as educators, parents, and mentors to provide support and encouragement to young people as they travel the path toward finding inner peace and discovering who they are. By working together, we will be able to assist them in achieving mental, physical, and spiritual success.

Chapter 14: Lifestyle Changes for Mental Wellness

Adolescence is a crucial stage of development that is characterized by fast changes in a person's physical appearance, cognitive abilities, and emotional state. At this point in time, it is of the utmost importance to encourage mental wellness in order to provide assistance to adolescents in overcoming the obstacles they are confronted with and to improve their overall quality of life. In this chapter, we look into the numerous lifestyle factors that have a profound influence on the mental health of adolescents and give measures that can be implemented to promote well-being among this population.

1. Adopting a Healthy Diet:

In order to create the groundwork for maximum mental wellness, it is important to encourage adolescents to adopt a diet that is balanced. For the purpose of maintaining brain health and regulating mood, a diet that is abundant in fruits, vegetables, whole grains, lean proteins, and healthy fats is an excellent source of critical nutrients. Consuming these meals provides the body with the vitamins, minerals, and antioxidants that are essential for the production of neurotransmitters and the proper functioning of the brain. On the other hand, consuming an excessive amount of processed foods, sugary snacks, and caffeine can cause fluctuations in energy levels and make mood swings even more severe. The mental and emotional well-being of teenagers can be positively impacted by providing them with the knowledge and tools necessary to make appropriate eating choices, as well as by educating them about the significance of nutrition.

2. Maintaining a Workout Routine:

Not only is physical activity excellent for one's physical health, but it also plays an important part in developing mental wellness if it is done regularly. The release of endorphins, which are neurotransmitters that are recognized for their ability to elevate one's mood, is stimulated by engaging in frequent physical activity. An further benefit of physical activity is that it lowers levels of stress hormones like cortisol and boosts the production of neurotransmitters like serotonin and dopamine, which are linked to emotions of happiness and pleasure. It is possible to greatly improve adolescents' mood, self-esteem, and overall mental health by encouraging them to incorporate exercise into their daily routine. This can be accomplished through playing sports, participating in outdoor activities, or participating in planned workouts.

A Sufficient Amount of Sleep:

For the sake of adolescents' mental health and cognitive functioning, making getting enough sleep a priority is absolutely necessary. Consolidating memories, processing feelings, and restoring energy levels are all things that the brain does while it is sleeping. The quality and duration of sleep can be improved by establishing a regular sleep pattern and practicing excellent sleep hygiene. This includes minimizing the amount of time spent in front of electronic screens before bedtime and developing a routine that is soothing before bedtime. A sufficient amount of sleep improves the ability of adolescents to maintain mental clarity, manage their emotions, and cope with stress, all of which contribute to an overall improvement in their well-being.

Fourth, Putting a Limit on Screen Time:
Excessive time spent in front of electronic screens, particularly in the hours leading up to bedtime, has the potential to alter the sleep habits of adolescents and have a severe influence on their mental health. The blue light that is emitted by screens inhibits the generation of melatonin,

which is a hormone that is necessary for the regulation of sleep-wake cycles. This results in a decrease in the quality of sleep as well as problems falling asleep completely. Relaxation and an overall improvement in mental well-being can be achieved by encouraging adolescents to restrict the amount of time they spend in front of screens and to participate in activities that take place away from the screen, such as reading, hobbies, or spending time with family and friends.

Using Technology with Mindfulness:
In spite of the fact that technology provides various advantages, such as connectivity and access to information, it is particularly important for adolescents to use it in a conscious manner. Excessive screen time can have negative impacts, but these effects can be mitigated by engaging in activities that enhance presence and connection with others, practicing digital detoxes, and taking breaks from screens. Fostering mindfulness, lowering feelings of stress and anxiety, and improving teenagers' general sense of well-being are all outcomes that can be achieved by encouraging them to build a good connection with any form of technology.

Sixth, Spending Time in Nature:

Adolescents have the opportunity to relax, reduce stress, and experience emotional regeneration when they spend time in natural settings. Those who spend time in natural areas, whether through activities that take place outside, treks through the woods, or simply taking in the splendor of the natural world, experience an increase in mental clarity, an improvement in mood, and a reduction in the symptoms of anxiety and depression. Motivating teenagers to develop a connection with nature helps them develop a sense of awe and appreciation for the environment around them, which in turn improves their overall well-being and enhances their resilience.

7. Relationships that are in good health:

It is essential for the mental health of adolescents to emphasize the importance of cultivating strong relationships with members of their family, friends, and other individuals who provide support. A sense of belonging, support, and acceptance are all provided by strong social relationships, which operate as a buffer against the adverse effects of stress and adversity. It is possible to promote emotional resilience in teenagers and boost their capacity to deal with the obstacles that life presents by encouraging them to cultivate meaningful relationships, communicate honestly, and seek support when they are in need of it.

It is possible for adolescents to improve their mental health and develop the resilience necessary to overcome the challenges that come with adolescence if they are encouraged to make adjustments to their lifestyles that are beneficial. It is possible for adolescents to build the skills and habits essential for sustaining optimal mental health and well-being by taking a holistic approach that includes nutrition, exercise, sleep, the use of technology, exposure to nature, and social interactions. We can help teenagers live lives that are meaningful and rewarding by empowering them to prioritize their mental health. This will allow them to have the resilience, optimism, and strength to live their lives to the fullest.

Chapter 15: Embracing Hope and Moving Forward

In the process of overcoming depression in young people, the acceptance of hope serves as a potent stimulant for the healing and development of the individual. The purpose of this final chapter is to discuss the significance of fostering hope and resiliency in teenagers, as well as to offer direction for going forward on the road to recovery.

Discovering Meaning in Difficult Circumstances

In life, we experience a sequence of highs and lows, and it is during the lows that we frequently discover the most important truths that we have to learn. It is possible to bring about a transformation by encouraging adolescents to view their challenges not as insurmountable obstacles but rather as chances for personal development and increased knowledge. It is possible for adolescents to nurture resilience and optimism in the face of adversity if they reframe obstacles as useful lessons and experiences that contribute to their personal development. Taking responsibility for the suffering while simultaneously embracing the opportunities for personal development that come with overcoming it is the key.

Goal-Setting That Is Based On Reality

A sense of purpose and direction can be gained from setting goals, particularly during difficult times. It is possible to empower adolescents to take control of their lives by assisting them in setting objectives for themselves that are both realistic and attainable. The process of defining and achieving objectives, whether they are small enough to be achieved on a daily basis or larger enough to be achieved over a longer period of time, provides a sense of accomplishment and progress. Because of this, individuals experience an increase in their self-esteem and motivation, which in turn reinforces the perception that they have the ability to influence their own future.

The Practice of Being Thankful

It is a potent antidote to despair to practice gratitude. The cultivation of thankfulness causes a shift in perspective, shifting our attention from what we do not have to appreciating what we do have. In order to assist adolescents in recognizing the positive parts of their lives, regardless of how insignificant they may be, it is beneficial to encourage them to keep a gratitude notebook or to engage in regular thankfulness rituals. Even in the face of challenging situations, it instills a sense of hope and appreciation in them, and it serves as a reminder that there is always something for which they should consider themselves grateful.

Keeping in Touch of Others

Because humans are social beings, having meaningful connections with other people is critical to maintaining emotional health. It is of the utmost importance to encourage adolescents to maintain connections with helpful individuals who offer them encouragement and inspiration. Maintaining these relationships, whether they be with friends, family members, mentors, or support groups, can serve as a source of encouragement, validation, and strength when going through challenging times. It can make a world of difference in how they see and approach their issues if they are aware that they are not the only ones going through what they are going through.

Seeking Assistance When It Is Required

The act of asking for assistance when one is in need of it is among the most courageous things a person can do. It is extremely important to remind adolescents that it is acceptable to seek support. Support and assistance can be obtained through a variety of channels, including but not limited to reaching out to a reliable adult, participating in therapy or counseling, or gaining access to community services. There is no indication of weakness in the act of seeking assistance; rather, it is a demonstration of strength and self-awareness. Having the fortitude to seek out further support and the ability to recognize when one's own resources are insufficient are both essential components of this principle.

Putting Self-Compassion into Practice

Compassion for oneself is frequently neglected, despite the fact that it is necessary for mental health. Motivating adolescents to treat themselves with kindness and compassion, particularly when they are going through difficult times or experiencing a setback, is extremely important. In order to practice self-compassion, one must treat themselves with the same level of understanding and care that they would extend to a close friend. In other words, it involves addressing flaws and errors with a compassionate and accepting attitude, rather than with self-criticism and condemnation. It is possible for adolescents to create a sense of inner peace and resilience via the practice of self-compassion, which empowers them to handle the challenges that they face in life with greater ease.

It is possible for adolescents to navigate the obstacles of youth depression with courage, fortitude, and resolve if they embrace optimism and resilience. They are getting closer to healing and rehabilitation with every step that they take, regardless of how small it may be. It is important to remind them that they are not alone and that better times are on the horizon as they continue on their respective journeys.

As a conclusion, let us reiterate our dedication to providing adolescents with support and empowerment as they travel the path toward mental heath and well-being throughout their lives. Let us work together to build a future in which every young person has the sense that they are appreciated, understood, and supported as they negotiate the complexity of adolescence and beyond.

www.ingramcontent.com/pod-product-compliance
Lightning Source LLC
LaVergne TN
LVHW020428080526
838202LV00055B/5084